D1406752

ILLINOIS PRAIRIE DPL

A65500 512153

# Experiments
# That
# Explore

## Acid Rain

# EXPERIMENTS THAT EXPLORE

# ACID RAIN

*An Investigate! Book*
*by Martin J. Gutnik*

*Illustrated by Sharon Lane Holm*
*The Millbrook Press*
*Brookfield, Connecticut*

ILLINOIS PRAIRIE DISTRICT LIBRARY

101665

Cover photograph courtesy of USDA/Forest Service
Photographs courtesy of: Photo Researchers: frontis (Karl H. Maslowski,
National Audubon Society), pp. 21 (William Curtsinger), 32 (top, Mary
M. Thacher), 45 (Stephen Collins), 61 (Gregory G. Dimijian); Adirondack
Museum: p. 8; AP/Wide World Photos: pp. 10–11, 44; UPI/Bettmann:
pp. 32 (bottom), 33, 46; USDA/Forest Service: p. 44.


Library of Congress Cataloging-in-Publication Data
Gutnik, Martin J.
Experiments that explore acid rain : an Investigate! book / by
Martin J. Gutnik.
p.   cm.
Includes bibliographical references and index.
Summary: Projects and experiments explore the causes and effects
of acid rain and ways of dealing with it.
ISBN 1-56294-115-1
1. Acid rain—Juvenile literature.   2. Acid rain—Experiments—
Juvenile literature.   [1. Acid rain—Experiments.
2. Experiments.]   I. Title.
TD195.44.G88   1992
628.5'32—dc20       91-19958 CIP AC

Copyright © 1992 by Martin J. Gutnik
All rights reserved
Printed in the United States of America
5   4   3   2   1

J
628.5
GUT
copy1

# *Contents*

5118.92 (13.21) Middbrook

*To Joseph Paul Luther*

*Special thanks to
Natalie Browne-Gutnik
for doing the primary
research for this book.*

# Experiments That Explore

## Acid Rain

*The Adirondacks contain many lakes
already severely affected by acid rain.*

# 1

## *Introduction*

New York State's Adirondack Mountains are made up of numerous low mountains, forests, streams, rivers, and lakes. They represent the largest remaining wilderness area in the United States east of the Mississippi River. With a permanent human population of only 125,000, the area remains largely untouched by human development. Yet this area of magnificent beauty is in trouble today. Its lakes and forests are dying. Approximately 8 percent of all the ponds and lakes in the Adirondack Mountains can support almost no life at all.

In Norway and Sweden, in areas far from industrial centers, the lakes are also dying. Approximately 20,000 of Sweden's 100,000 lakes are already dead. Why?

The problem is *acid rain,* a form of air and water pollution resulting from toxic emissions (poisonous gases and particles released into the air) by industry, transportation, and home heating. Besides threatening the lakes of the United States, Canada, and Europe, acid rain also poses a threat to their forests, farmlands, soils, and buildings.

Acid rain is one of the most significant environmental threats to face the people of the world today. How we deal with this problem will have a major impact on future generations.

People have created the acid rain problem. Factories, transportation systems, and electrical and heating plants all release tremendous quantities of toxic particles and gases such as sulfur dioxide ($SO_2$) and nitrogen oxides into our atmosphere. Most of the particles float in the air for a while and later fall back to Earth. Others rise higher in the air and combine with moisture in the clouds to form sulfuric acid ($H_2SO_4$) and nitric acid ($HNO_3$). As the clouds become laden with this toxic moisture,

they release their liquid burden, which falls back to Earth in the form of rain, snow, sleet, hail, or fog. Carried by the wind, these toxic substances can travel great distances, affecting areas far from the source. This liquid fallout is what is known as acid rain.

*Our transportation systems add greatly to the acid-rain problem.*

The effects of acid rain are so far-reaching and so devastating that something must be done about it immediately. Acid rain pollution has already affected over one million square miles of the North American continent. Some forms of wildlife have already been severely affected. Tens of thousands of lakes are nearly dead, and many more are in danger. The soil is also affected by acid rain and, through the soil, so are trees and other plants. Buildings and monuments, too, are subject to damage from this pollution. Finally, there is evidence that acid rain is responsible for some human health problems.

What can be done to stop the devastation? Is the future without hope? No! The acid rain problem was created by people, and it can be corrected by people. We need only the knowledge and the will to move forward.

The first step is understanding the problem. The projects that follow will demonstrate the makeup of certain aspects of the environment and the impact that acid rain has on them. When you are finished with this book, you will have a much clearer understanding of this environmental hazard.

All of the experiments in this book are designed to demonstrate natural events and the interactions between various parts of the natural environment. Some experiments will show the harmful effects of acid rain. Several of these experiments are potentially dangerous. Special care must be taken by the experimenter. These experiments should be done *only* with an adult present.

## THE PROCESS OF SCIENCE (SCIENTIFIC METHOD)

From the beginnings of formal scientific investigation, scientists have followed certain organized procedures in performing their work. These procedures have helped them to conduct their experiments with accuracy and little repetition. They have also aided scientists in coming to logical conclusions based on facts uncovered during their investigation. These procedures have collectively come to be known as the *scientific method.*

The scientific method of investigation consists of a series of orderly steps that help scientists, or any other investigators, solve problems. The first step in this process is *observation.* Observation is basic to any type of investigation. It involves using all of your senses plus researching the available scientific literature to find out all you can about an object or event.

Human beings have five senses: sight, touch, hearing, smell, and taste. All of these senses may be helpful when attempting to understand some unusual phenomena. Not all of these senses are used, however, in every investigation. Quite often, scientists or other investigators, such as the police, use tools to enhance their senses. For example, microscopes help researchers see a world not visible to the naked eye. Physicians use many specialized tools, such as X-ray machines, to help them observe the functions of the human body.

Another step in the scientific method is known as *classification.* Classification means putting objects into meaningful groups. Objects are classified according to their properties. A *property* is something that belongs to an object that helps us to identify that object. A property common to all mammals, for example, is warm-bloodedness. All reptiles are cold-blooded. It follows then that humans, who are mammals, would be classified in one group, while snakes, which are reptiles, would be classified in another.

After observing and classifying an event, the scientist will use this information to make an *inference* or a *prediction.* An inference is a statement, based upon what has been observed and classified, about something that *has happened.* A prediction is a statement, based upon what has been observed and classified, about something that is *going to happen.*

Inferences and predictions are only as accurate as the information upon which they are based. The more information an investigator has gathered, the more likely that the inference or prediction will be correct.

13

Inferences are very useful to physicians or laboratory technicians investigating the cause of a disease. Predictions are helpful in designing vaccines.

Once the researcher has made an inference or a prediction, he or she must put it in a statement that can be tested. This statement is referred to as the *hypothesis*. The hypothesis is the most important part of the scientific investigation. All things done while performing an experiment must refer back to the hypothesis. A hypothesis usually takes the form of an ''if-then'' statement (for example: If human beings are mammals, then they must be warm-blooded).

With the hypothesis formulated, the investigator may now conduct the experiment. Most scientists and other researchers keep a record of all the materials and methods used while conducting the experiment. In doing this, they ensure that other people investigating the same subject will be aware of the procedures used. They also must do this in case they have to do the experiment over. By having all the information recorded, it is easier to discover if anything was done incorrectly or if a step was missed.

After the testing is completed, all the *results* must be recorded. These results are then studied to see if the outcomes of the experiment were as predicted or inferred.

Finally, after the results are recorded and analyzed, the investigator is ready to draw *conclusions*. Conclusions must state whether you proved or disproved the hypothesis. They must also tell why your hypothesis was correct or incorrect.

Your conclusions may not always be valid. This is because of *variables* that cannot be controlled. Variables are differing conditions that may affect the results of your experiment. It is important to state the variables in your conclusion so that others can better analyze the results of your investigation.

Many times an experiment will not prove or disprove the hypothesis. This does not mean that the experiment failed. Rather, it indicates the need for further investigation. The researcher should restate his or her hypothesis and investigate the problem further.

# THE FORMAL REPORT

All science projects are more useful when they are accompanied by a written report saying exactly what was done during the experiment. The write-up should read somewhat like a recipe. This will allow other investigators to use your methods and discoveries for their own research.

Quite often your written report will be used to conduct further investigations based on a new problem that was identified during your experiment. Without a written log of what was done, it would be difficult to set up the same situation again.

# 2

## Nature's Cycles

*Ecology* is the study of how all living things interrelate to each other and to their nonliving environment. The planet Earth can be divided into two aspects: the *biological* and the *physical*. The biological aspect refers to all living things and to all things that were or will be living. Therefore, an egg is biological, as is a rotting log. Physical refers to the nonliving parts of the environment. The physical aspect includes air, water, soil (sand, gravel, earth, clay, and rock), and energy.

The *biosphere* is anywhere on Earth where air, water, soil, and energy are in a proper mix for life to flourish. It is within the biosphere that all of the complex relationships between the physical and biological worlds occur.

Nature, with its natural cycles, has always maintained a delicate balance within the biosphere. It was not until recently that this balance was threatened. Some of the activities of people—masses of people— now threaten the very relationships that support life on our planet. Like a parasite that destroys its host, people are in the process of destroying their only life support system—the environment.

Acid rain, a pollutant created mostly through the activities of people, threatens all of the physical parts of the biosphere. Through them, the biological aspect is threatened. The destruction of our air, water, and soil must be stopped before it becomes impossible to reverse.

## Science Project #1—
## Interrelationships: Living to Nonliving

### Materials Needed

5 potted coleus, ajuga, or other green plants
5 bell jars or large mayonnaise jars
large medicine cup or small jar

masking tape (for labeling jars)
pen or pencil
soda lime crystals (to absorb carbon dioxide)

(NOTE: This is a *controlled experiment*. In a controlled experiment, the experimenter attempts to control all the variables. This helps the researcher to analyze the results.)

*Observations and Classifications.* As was stated previously, all living things need air, water, soil, and energy (especially light energy) in order to exist. If any one of these four physical elements is missing, then life cannot exist.

*Inference.* Without air, water, soil, and light energy, living things cannot exist.

*Hypothesis.* If a green plant is denied air, water, soil, or light energy, then it will sicken and eventually die.

*Procedure.* Set one of your plants in its pot on a windowsill or any other place where there is adequate light. Water it, and cover it with one of the bell or mayonnaise jars. Label this plant *A—Control.* Water another plant, cover it with a jar, and put it on the windowsill. Place a medicine cup filled with soda lime crystals in the jar. Soda lime crystals absorb $CO_2$. Label this plant *B—No $CO_2$* (no carbon dioxide). Since this plant will not be receiving air, it will also not be receiving any carbon dioxide, which is a gas found in air.

Take the soil out of one of the remaining pots and place its plant back in the pot without soil. Water it, and cover it with another jar. Label this plant *C—No Soil.*

Take another of the remaining plants, place it with the others, and cover it with a jar without watering it. Label this plant *D—No Water.*

Finally, take the last plant, water it, and put it in a closet or cabinet where there is no light. Cover this plant with a jar, and label it *E—No Light.*

Allow the plants to stand for approximately one month. Water those that are supposed to receive water once each week. Also check all the plants at least once each week, and log the progress of your experiment in your results.

***Results.*** Plants B, C, D, and E are all dead or dying because they are missing at least one of the four physical elements required to support life.

***Conclusion.*** My hypothesis was correct because all of the plants missing an element died. The only plant that lived and remained healthy was the plant that received air, water, soil, and light energy.

(NOTE: From this point on, conclusions to projects will be given in a separate section at the end of this book.)

## THE FOOD WEBS

Most living things are interrelated through the *grazing food web* (all the various food relationships within a specific environment). The food web is the natural method for transferring and transforming energy throughout an environment.

All food webs begin with green plants. Green plants are the only living things on Earth that can convert light energy into chemical energy in order to make food. They do this through the process of *photosyn-*

## Chart of Results

| | A | B | C | D | E |
|---|---|---|---|---|---|
| Week 1 | Doing Fine | Doing Fine | Withered | Doing Fine | Doing Fine |
| Week 2 | Doing Fine | Losing Some Color | Shriveled Up | Withering | Losing Some Color |
| Week 3 | | | | | |
| Week 4 | | | | | |

**(MAKE YOUR OWN CHART OR PHOTOCOPY THIS ONE.)**

*thesis*. The food they make is a simple sugar called *glucose*. They store this glucose and convert it to fats, proteins, and carbohydrates. Without green plants, there would be no food on Earth.

The next level in the grazing food web is made up of *herbivores*. Herbivores are animals that eat only green plants. They can convert the energy stores in plants into energy for themselves. Herbivores are an important link in the food relationships of an environment. Without them, the energy could not be transferred from plants to most other living things, which must eat meat to live. Herbivores are found in every environment on Earth. Some examples of herbivores are elephants, cows, giraffes, certain insects and fish, blue whales, antelope, prairie dogs, and squirrels.

*Carnivores,* animals that eat only meat (herbivores or other carnivores), form the third level of the grazing food web. These animals are predators. They must hunt and kill prey in order to exist. Carnivores perform an important function in the grazing food web. They limit the number of herbivores. If there were too many herbivores, all the green plants would be eaten, and then the food web would be destroyed.

There are many kinds of carnivores. A number of species of reptile and amphibian eat only herbivores. Other carnivores eat herbivores and other carnivores. Some of this type are wolves, lions, jaguars, coyotes, dogs, cats, weasels, badgers, cheetahs, bass, northern pike, and praying mantises.

Other members of the grazing food web are animals called *omnivores*. The word *omnivore* comes from *omni,* the Greek word meaning ''all.'' Omnivores eat both meat and plants and can be found everywhere within the grazing food web. Some omnivores are people, bears, raccoons, and turtles.

Everything that lives produces waste and eventually dies. What happens to all of the decaying and waste material? It is converted into energy through the *detritus food web*. The detritus food web consists of plants and animals that eat decaying or waste materials, convert them into nitrates, and return these to the soil to be used again in the grazing food

*Turtles, an important part of nature's food web, are seriously threatened by acid rain, which kills off plants and small fish in the turtle's natural habitat.*

# Food Web in a Pond

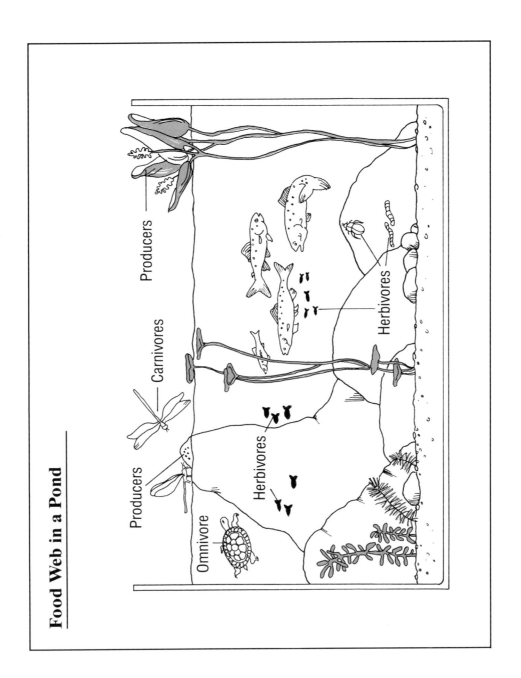

web. Plants and animals in this food web consist of certain worms, flies, fungi, and bacteria.

As we said earlier, everything in nature is interrelated. Thus, changing any element in the food web will eventually affect all the other elements.

## Science Project #2—
## Interrelationships: Living to Living

### Materials Needed

| | |
|---|---|
| binoculars | pad of paper |
| markers, crayons, or colored pencils | pen or pencil |

*Observations and Classifications.* Observations and classifications on food webs have been obtained from reading about food webs in the sections above.

*Inference.* There are many specific environments (*ecosystems*) on Earth that have food webs.

*Hypothesis.* If there is life within a specific ecosystem, then there must be a food web to transfer energy throughout the system.

*Procedure.* Go out into your community and find a specific ecosystem: a marsh, woodland, or similar environment. Observe the ecosystem for several hours each day over many days. Diagram and label the food relationships in the ecosystem you observed.

# 3

## What Is
## an Acid?

An *acid* is any substance with a sour taste. It turns blue litmus paper red. Litmus paper is treated with a dye obtained from a lichen plant. A *base,* or *alkaline* substance, reacts with an acid to form a salt. Bases turn red litmus paper blue. Bases feel slippery when rubbed between your fingers, and they have a bitter taste.

Most acids contain hydrogen (H), and strong acids are very *corrosive*. This means that they eat away at substances with which they come in contact. Acids react with bases to form *salts*. When an acid and a base react to form a salt, it is called *neutralization*. The reaction neutralizes the acid and the base. Water, as well as a salt, is one of the products of neutralization.

Many substances on Earth contain acids. Rainwater is a naturally mild acid (carbonic acid, $H_2CO_3$). Citrus fruits, such as oranges, grapefruits, and lemons, contain citric acid ($C_6H_8O_7$). Milk contains lactic acid ($CH_3CHOHCOOH$), vinegar contains acetic acid ($CH_3COOH$), and apples contain malic acid ($C_4H_6O_5$).

All bases are *hydroxyls*. A hydroxyl (OH) is an oxygen atom (O) and a hydrogen atom (H) chemically bound together. One common base is ammonium hydroxide ($NH_4OH$), which is often referred to simply as ammonia. Ammonia is used to clean windows and other household surfaces. Calcium hydroxide (Ca(OH)$_2$), another common base also called limewater, is used in mixing mortar for cement. It is also used in chemistry experiments as a carbon dioxide indicator.

The *pH scale* is used for measuring the level of acidity or alkalinity of substances. According to this scale, any substance that has a pH of 7.0 is neutral; below 7.0 is acidic; and above 7.0 is basic, or alkaline. Changes in pH are on a logarithmic scale, so a pH of 3 is ten times more acidic than a pH of 4 and one hundred times more acidic than a pH of 5.

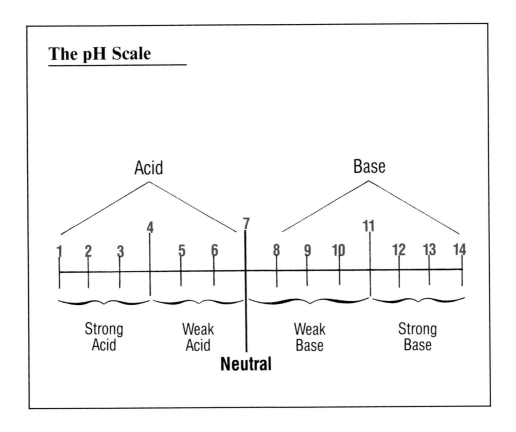

**The pH Scale**

# Science Project #3—
## Identifying Acids and Bases

### Materials Needed

test tubes, medicine cups, or small jars

test tube rack (if using test tubes)

ammonium hydroxide

apple juice

boric acid

lemon juice

limewater

milk

tap water

vinegar

masking tape (for labeling test tubes)

litmus paper (red and blue)

pad of paper

pen or pencil

(NOTE: Some of the equipment and many of the chemicals used here and in other experiments in this book can be obtained from your school's science department. AMMONIUM HYDROXIDE IS POISONOUS AND HARMFUL TO TOUCH. Do not taste it, and be sure to wash your hands after the experiment. Do the experiment ONLY with an adult present.

Though limewater and boric acid are not as dangerous to handle, they are still chemicals. It is a good practice not to taste or touch *any* chemical.)

***Observations and Classifications.*** Observations and classifications on acids and bases have been obtained from reading about acids and bases in this chapter. A substance is classified as an acid, a base, or neutral according to where it falls on the pH scale. All substances on Earth are either acid, base, or neutral.

***Prediction.*** Acids will turn blue litmus paper red, while bases will turn red litmus paper blue.

***Hypothesis.*** If we test various substances with litmus paper, then acidic substances will turn the blue litmus paper red, alkaline substances will turn the red litmus paper blue, and neutral substances will not change the color of either litmus paper.

26

*Procedure.* Fill each test tube (use a medicine cup or a small jar if a test tube is not available) with one of the chemical substances listed in the *Materials Needed* section of this project. Label each test tube with the name or chemical formula of the substance in it.

Test each substance with a separate piece of litmus paper, and immediately record the results on a chart. Examine the results of the experiment and form your conclusion.

*Results.* 1. The apple juice, boric acid, lemon juice, milk, and vinegar turned the blue litmus paper red, indicating acid. 2. The ammonium hydroxide and limewater turned the red litmus paper blue, indicating a base. 3. The tap water did not change the color of either piece of litmus paper, indicating neutral.

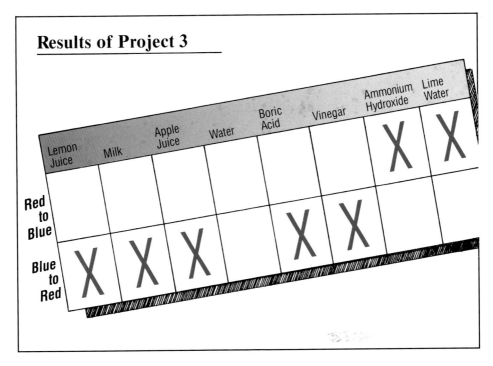

**Results of Project 3**

101665

ILLINOIS PRAIRIE DISTRICT LIBRARY

## Science Project #4—
## Acids and Bases Neutralize One Another

### Materials Needed

beaker

litmus paper (red and blue)

masking tape (for labeling beaker
  and jars)

pad of paper

pen or pencil

safety goggles

sodium hydroxide

tablespoon

medicine dropper

2 small jars

vinegar

(NOTE: This project uses the chemical sodium hydroxide, which is potentially dangerous. Conduct this experiment ONLY with an adult present, be sure to wear safety goggles, and carefully read the warnings on the sodium hydroxide bottle.)

*Observations and Classifications.* When an acid and a base are mixed, they neutralize one another. The formula for this reaction is:

$$acid + base = neutral$$

*Prediction.* An acid and a base mixed together in proper proportions will neutralize one another.

*Hypothesis.* If vinegar (acetic acid) is combined with sodium hydroxide (NaOH), then they will neutralize one another.

*Procedure.* Ask your science teacher for the sodium hydroxide. Pour the solution into one small jar and label this jar *NaOH*. Pour the solution of vinegar into the other jar, and label that jar *vinegar*.

Test each solution with red and blue litmus paper by dipping the paper into the solution and watching for a reaction. Record the results.

Pour a tablespoon of sodium hydroxide into a small beaker. Now, using the medicine dropper, add the vinegar, drop by drop, to the sodium hydroxide solution. Test the solution with litmus paper each time a drop of vinegar is added. Record the results. Keep adding the vinegar until you reach the point where the litmus paper no longer changes color. Record how many drops of vinegar it took until the paper no longer changed color. Is the base neutralized?

Set the beaker of neutralized solution on a windowsill or in another dry area. Be sure to label it "POISONOUS" so that no one touches it. Put the beaker well out of reach of young children. Allow the jar to stand for approximately one week, observing it daily. What happens when the solution finally evaporates? Record this in your results.

*Results.* 1. The acid (vinegar) turned the blue litmus paper red. 2. The base (NaOH) turned the red litmus paper blue. 3. The base was neutralized by the acid. 4. When the neutralized solution evaporated, there were crystals of salt on the bottom of the beaker.

## Science Project #5—
## The Corrosiveness of Acids

### Materials Needed

beaker or small jar
vinegar or lemon juice concentrate
additional materials for testing:
    cotton cloth, unfinished wood,
    a brick, a plastic container, an
    aluminum pot
pad of paper, pen or pencil

medicine dropper
a bathroom tile, preferably black
    (This may be obtained from
    any tile store and from most
    building-supply stores. Black
    is preferred because it will be
    easier to observe the results.)

*Observations and Classifications.* A strong acid, 1 to 3 on the pH scale, can be highly corrosive. For example, the hydrochloric acid in your stomach is strong enough to break down most of the foods that you eat. If a drop of human stomach acid were placed on a brick or countertop, it would eat its way through the surface of the material in very little time. Even weak acids will corrode some surfaces. Because of the corrosive nature of acids, they are often used in industry as solvents (dissolvers).

*Inference.*   An acid has the ability to corrode many substances.

*Hypothesis.*   If even a weak acid has the ability to cause corrosion, then acid dropped from a medicine dropper onto certain substances will corrode those substances.

*Procedure.*   Pour a solution of vinegar or lemon juice concentrate into a beaker or small jar. Fill a medicine dropper with some of the acid and drop it, one drop at a time, onto the tile. Watch what happens and record the results. Repeat this process every day for the next week. After that time, describe what happened to the tile in your results. Test the other materials and describe what happened to them.

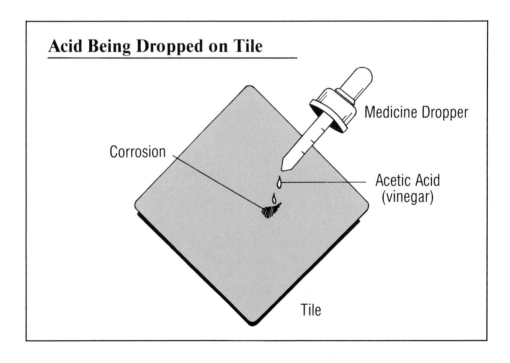

**Acid Being Dropped on Tile**

Medicine Dropper

Corrosion

Acetic Acid (vinegar)

Tile

# 4

## *Acid Rain: How It Forms and Where It Comes From*

## NATURAL CAUSES

Nature itself contributes to pollution problems worldwide. This is called *natural pollution*. However, pollutants produced by nature, such as gases from volcanic eruptions, are easily absorbed by the vastness of the Earth. There is no permanent damage to the environment. Nature's polluting activities are simply part of its building activities.

Acid rain results in part from emissions of sulfur gases into the air. In nature, rotting swamps produce the gas hydrogen sulfide ($H_2S$). This gas, a noxious-smelling substance, rises into the air. It combines with water vapor and forms sulfuric acid.

Volcanoes, when they erupt, produce tremendous quantities of sulfur dioxide gas. This gas also combines with water vapor in the air to produce sulfuric acid. The sulfuric acid is then borne by the wind to various parts of the Earth. Eventually clouds form, become laden with moisture, and then release this moisture in the form of rain, sleet, or snow into the environment. This is acid rain.

The acid rain from volcanic eruptions and swamps is the same as the acid rain produced by the activities of people. Its effects, although potentially the same as those from human-produced acid rain, are not nearly as devastating. This is because the natural emissions that cause acid rain are usually short-lived and confined to smaller areas.

*Rotting swamps and volcanoes
are sources of natural pollution.*

## THE ACTIVITIES OF PEOPLE

It starts with industry. Smokestacks from factories and power plants belch their sulfuric emissions into the air. Along with this, millions of automobiles, buses, trucks, and planes emit billions of tons of invisible gases into our air. These gases, among them the oxides of nitrogen as well as sulfur dioxide, drift into the atmosphere and, carried on the wind, spread across vast areas of the planet.

*Smokestacks from factories such as this one, with no pollution controls, were common in the 1950s and 1960s. There are fewer today, but the release of polluting substances into the air is still a major problem.*

The wilderness areas most greatly affected lie near industrial centers, downwind from power plants and urban areas. These tracts of land usually receive lots of rain. They are very susceptible to the subtlest changes in their environmental makeup.

Sulfur dioxide gas causes approximately 70 percent of the acid rain problem; nitrogen oxides cause the rest. The sulfur dioxide comes mostly from power plants and industries that use coal and oil as their main fuel. In Eastern Europe, where soft, high-sulfur coal is the main fuel, the sulfur dioxide emissions have reached extremely dangerous levels.

In the United States, sulfur dioxide emissions come mainly from electrical power plants that use fossil fuels (mainly coal and oil) as their energy source. In areas such as the Ohio River valley, high-sulfur coal is burned with minimum effort to control the sulfur dioxide emissions.

The United States is the largest producer of sulfur dioxide in the world, emitting approximately 30 million tons a year. Most of the toxic particles drift on the prevailing winds and fall back to the Earth within a few hundred to one thousand miles from their source. In North America, the deadly breezes usually blow northeast, carrying the acid-laden clouds over the East Coast of the United States and into southeastern Canada. In Europe, the prevailing winds carry the sulfur dioxide produced in Western and Eastern Europe to Scandinavia.

Nitrogen oxides are produced mainly by the transportation systems of modern society. These deadly chemicals spew from the exhaust pipes of automobiles, trucks, and buses, and they are carried around the world by the winds.

## THE TWO TYPES OF
## ACID DEPOSITION

The winds carry the sulfur dioxide and nitrogen oxides to various parts of the globe. These acidic chemicals eventually fall back to Earth. This is called *deposition*.

*Wet deposition:* As the sulfur dioxide and nitrous oxides rise into the atmosphere, they combine with water vapor to form sulfuric acid and nitric acid. These acids fall back to Earth as rain, snow, sleet, or hail.

*Dry deposition:* Some of the sulfur and nitrogen compounds fall back to Earth before they have had a chance to combine with water vapor in the air. These particles stay on the ground and are potential producers of acids, combining with water when the rains or snows eventually come. They also combine with surface water to form the acidic compounds mentioned above. Dry deposition is as harmful as wet deposition, and it causes at least 30 percent of the acid rain problem.

## Science Project #6— Producing Sulfur Dioxide ($SO_2$)

### Materials Needed

| | |
|---|---|
| alcohol burner or candle | ring stand |
| lead acetate test paper | small metal dish |
| matches | sulfur |
| slivers of paraffin wax | tablespoon |
| pitcher of water | tongs or tweezers |

(NOTE: Perform this experiment ONLY with an adult present. Also, conduct the experiment in a well-ventilated room.)

*Observations and Classifications.*   Sulfur dioxide gas is created by the burning of high-sulfur fuels. The sulfur is released, and it combines with oxygen in the atmosphere to form sulfur dioxide gas. This is a colorless, tasteless, heavier-than-air gas. It can be harmful to people and animals. When breathed in, it can irritate the linings of the nose, throat, and lungs. When combined with water, it forms sulfuric acid. Lead acetate test paper in the presence of water and sulfur dioxide gas turns from white to gray or brownish gray.

*Inference.*   When sulfur is burned, it combines with oxygen in the air to produce sulfur dioxide gas.

*Hypothesis.*   If sulfur is burned, then it will combine with oxygen in the air to form sulfur dioxide gas.

*Procedure.*   Set up your ring stand to hold the small metal dish. Set the alcohol burner or candle under the ring so that the flame will reach the bottom of the metal dish.

Put two tablespoons of sulfur into the metal dish and add some slivers of paraffin wax to the sulfur. Light your alcohol burner and wait while the flame melts the sulfur and paraffin wax. After the sulfur has melted, it will start to produce sulfur dioxide gas. Using tongs, place a piece of moistened lead acetate test paper into the smoke and fumes of the gas. What happens to the paper? Write down your answer in the results.

Blow out the alcohol burner. Put the flames in the sulfur out by pouring some water into the metal dish. Afterward, lift the dish with the tongs and place it in a sink. Run water into the dish to make certain that the flame is out.

*Results.*   The lead acetate paper turned gray.

## Science Project #7— Making Acid Rain

*Materials Needed*

ring stand
small metal dish
tablespoon
sulfur
slivers of paraffin wax
alcohol burner or candle
litmus paper (blue)
masking tape (for taping litmus
    paper onto glass)

small pane of glass or mirror (about
    4″ × 4″)
matches
atomizer bottle with bulb squeeze
    pump or handle pump (An
    old, cleaned Windex bottle
    will do. Be sure to wash the
    bottle thoroughly.)
tongs or tweezers

(NOTE: Perform this experiment ONLY with an adult present. Also, conduct the experiment in a well-ventilated room.)

## Producing Sulfur Dioxide Gas

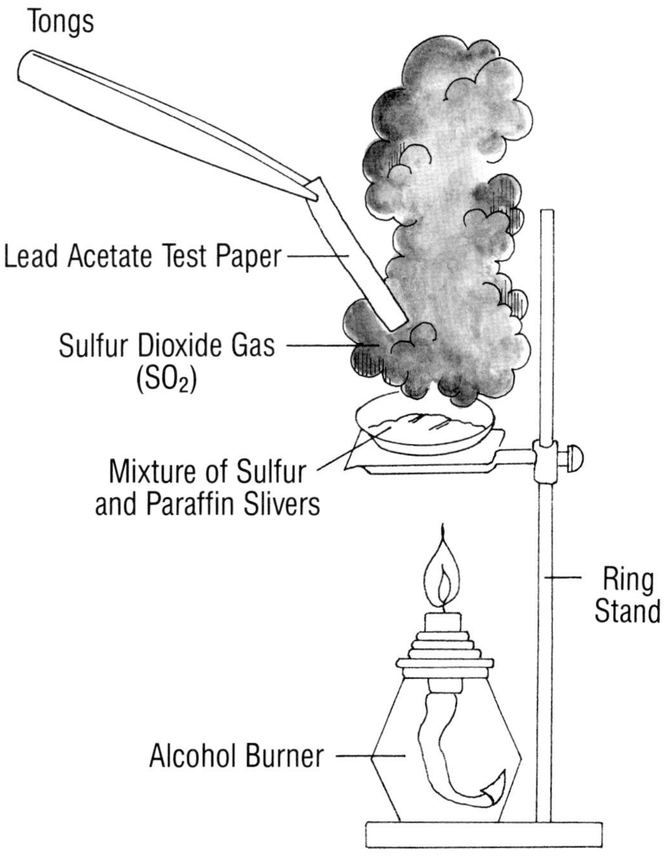

Tongs

Lead Acetate Test Paper

Sulfur Dioxide Gas
(SO$_2$)

Mixture of Sulfur
and Paraffin Slivers

Ring
Stand

Alcohol Burner

*Observations and Classifications.*  Observations and classifications for this experiment have been obtained by reading the earlier sections of this chapter.

*Inference.*  When sulfur dioxide gas combines with water vapor, it will produce sulfuric acid.

*Hypothesis.*  If sulfur dioxide gas is combined with water vapor, then sulfuric acid will be produced.

*Procedure.*  Set up your ring stand, metal dish, sulfur, paraffin, and alcohol burner in the same manner as described in Science Project #6. Tape three strips of blue litmus paper onto the pane of glass or mirror.

Light the alcohol burner and melt three tablespoons of the sulfur plus a few slivers of paraffin wax. After the sulfur and paraffin have melted, they will generate sulfur dioxide gas. Hold the pane of glass on one side of the smoke and fumes and, using the atomizer, spray water through the smoke and fumes onto the blue litmus paper. Once the litmus paper has changed color, blow out the alcohol burner and put out the fire by spraying water onto the flames. Using your tongs, lift the dish off the ring stand and put it in the sink. Run water into the dish to make certain that the fire is out. Record the results of your experiment.

*Results.*  The blue litmus paper turned red.

## Science Project #8— Monitoring Acid Rain

### Materials Needed

construction paper or tagboard
marking pen
ruler (for making lines on chart)
water pH test kit

rain gauge (This collector can be bought at most hardware or garden-supply stores.)
tweezers

# Making Acid Rain

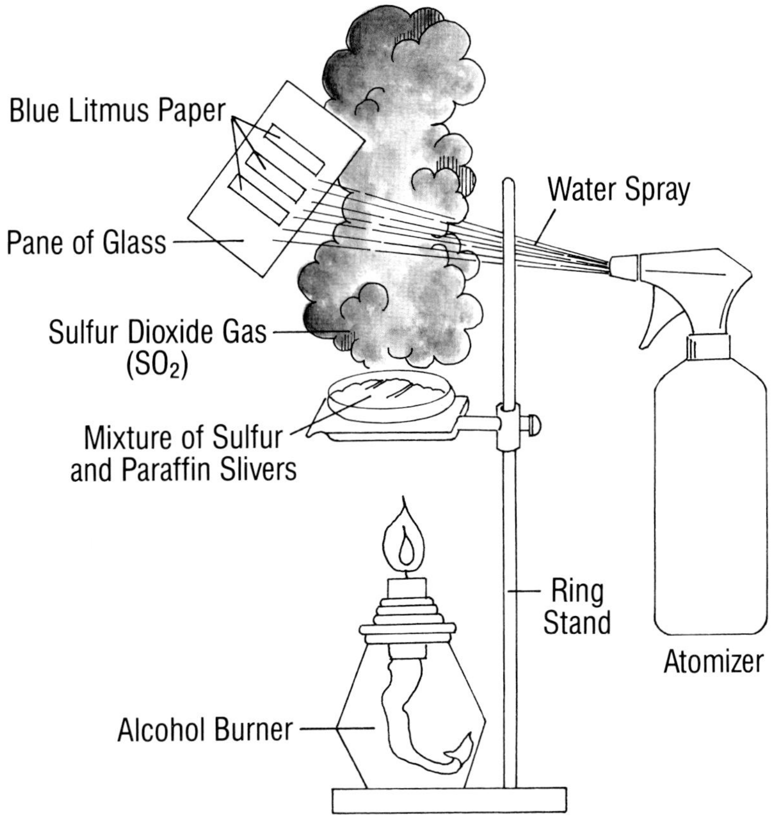

Blue Litmus Paper

Pane of Glass

Water Spray

Sulfur Dioxide Gas ($SO_2$)

Mixture of Sulfur and Paraffin Slivers

Ring Stand

Atomizer

Alcohol Burner

***Observations and Classifications.*** Normal rainwater is slightly acidic, about 5.6 on the pH scale. This is because carbon dioxide gas in the air combines with water vapor to form carbonic acid. Rainwater, because of its acidity, is called *soft water*. This normal, slightly acidic quality of rainwater has no harmful effects on the environment.

Acid rain measures anywhere from about 3.5 to 5.5 on the pH scale and falls in the form of nitric or sulfuric acid. This is not normal and has been shown to have a harmful impact on the environment.

***Prediction.*** Acid rain will measure from approximately 3.5 to 5.5 on the pH scale.

***Hypothesis.*** If rainfall is truly acid rain and not just normally acidic, then it will measure less than 5.6 on the pH scale.

***Procedure.*** Set up your monitoring station somewhere in your backyard or school yard. Rainwater is very easily contaminated by foreign substances. Thus, find an area for your rain gauge where there is very little else around to contaminate the water. Some good places are on a roof, in the middle of an open area, on a fence, and always away from trees.

Make a rain gauge chart on a sheet of tagboard or construction paper. This chart will be used for one month to record all of your observations on weather conditions, such as precipitation and wind speed. (The weather conditions in this experiment are variables that may affect the outcome.)

When putting data onto the chart, be as specific as you can. For example, put down the exact wind speed for the day. Describe whether it is a cloudy or a sunny day.

Follow these steps daily:

1. Each day at the same time, before recording on your chart, call your local weather information number or listen to the radio to get the current temperature and wind speed and the forecast for the day. Put this information on your chart. Check your newspaper for the previous day's conditions if you need to.

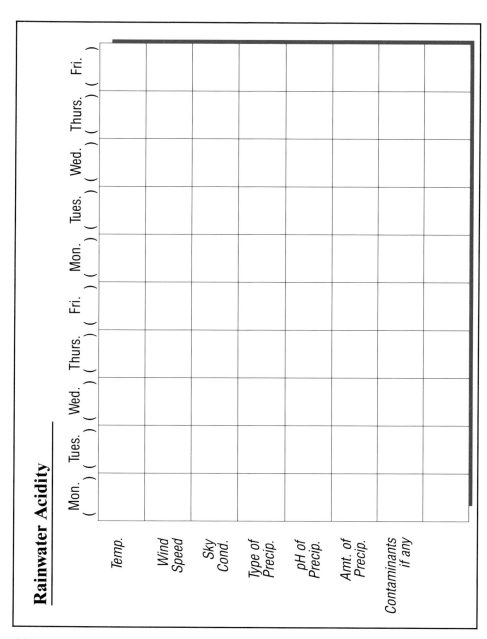

**Rainwater Acidity**

| | Mon. ( ) | Tues. ( ) | Wed. ( ) | Thurs. ( ) | Fri. ( ) | Mon. ( ) | Tues. ( ) | Wed. ( ) | Thurs. ( ) | Fri. ( ) |
|---|---|---|---|---|---|---|---|---|---|---|
| Temp. | | | | | | | | | | |
| Wind Speed | | | | | | | | | | |
| Sky Cond. | | | | | | | | | | |
| Type of Precip. | | | | | | | | | | |
| pH of Precip. | | | | | | | | | | |
| Amt. of Precip. | | | | | | | | | | |
| Contaminants if any | | | | | | | | | | |

**(MAKE YOUR OWN CHART OR PHOTOCOPY THIS ONE.)**

41

2. Go to the rain gauge and determine the type and amount of precipitation, if any, that fell the previous day and during the night. Record this on a sheet of paper. Later, when you are in your classroom or at home, you can transfer this information to the chart.

3. Check the precipitation for pH by putting a strip of pH test paper in the liquid that has collected in the rain gauge. Hold the test paper with a tweezers, so that the strip is not contaminated by the chemicals from your hands. Hold the paper in the liquid for two to three minutes. Remove the pH strip from the liquid and compare its color to the color on your pH color chart (this chart should have come with the pH test kit). Record the pH on a sheet of paper. Later, transfer this information onto your chart.

4. Empty the collector, rinsing it if possible, and put it back in place for the next day. Even if it did not rain the previous day, rinse out the rain gauge to make certain that it does not have any debris in it that may contaminate the rainwater.

After one month, analyze your results and state your conclusions.

# 5

## *The Effects of Acid Rain*

In 1852, English chemist Robert Angus Smith linked the coal-sooted skies of Manchester, England, with the erosion of buildings in the city. After testing the precipitation, he found that its acidic content was much higher than normal. He wrote a paper about this relationship and referred to the precipitation as *acid rain*. Robert Angus Smith was the first person to use the term.

It was not until the late 1960s that the term acid rain was revived. It was used to refer to the acidic precipitation that fell across the northeastern United States and southeastern Canada. This was when scientists and environmental activists first became concerned about the effects of polluted rainfall.

In the late 1970s, a network was set up all across North America to track the culprits. These monitoring stations were part of the United States' National Atmospheric Deposition Program and the Canadian Network for Sampling Precipitation. Together, these programs collected samples of rain from thirty-two states and fifty-five locations in Canada.

The results of this monitoring revealed that large portions of the United States and Canada were experiencing very highly acidic precipitation. These rains averaged 4.0 on the pH scale.

As acid rain falls, it changes the makeup of the soil by *leaching* (washing away) important nutrient salts and traces of metals. Trees need these salts and metals in order to live. The trees of the forest try to

*In this acid-rain study, a lake in Wyoming
is being surveyed for its level of acidity.*

compensate for this loss by releasing hydrogen into the soil. The hydrogen further acidifies the soil, causing further leaching of important salts and metals. As the process continues, the trees' roots are eventually deprived of nutrients such as calcium, potassium, and aluminum.

As the rains continue to fall, the leached metals, salts, and acids flow into the rivers and lakes, changing the chemical makeup of the water. Aluminum, one of the leached metals, collects in the gills of the fish. This is irritating to the fish and causes them to produce mucus in order to combat the irritant. In fry (baby fish), so much mucus is produced that it eventually strangles them.

Acid rainfall does not destroy a lake in a short time. Rather, it is the buildup of pollutants over time that eventually destroys the lake's ability to neutralize the acid. After years of this rain, the entire makeup of the lake is altered. The crustaceans (snails, clams, and crayfish) are the first species to be affected, and then the aquatic insects (mayflies, dragonflies, and stone flies). After this, the amphibians (frogs and salamanders) begin to die, then the reptiles (snakes and turtles), and eventually the fish. Amphibians are especially affected by acid rain because they lay their eggs in shallow pools. These pools become highly acidic during the spring rains.

*Amphibians, such as this wood frog, lay their eggs in shallow ponds that are frequently highly acidic. The eggs do not hatch, and the result is often a drastic decrease in reproduction rates.*

The buildup of acid in a lake harms the fish in many different ways. Aluminum leached from the soil by acid rain clogs the fish's gills; a lowering in the pH alters the breeding grounds so that many species cannot reproduce; and, due to the leaching process, the fish are deprived of calcium. When the fish do not get enough calcium, their bones are weakened, and their bodies become deformed. They also have difficulty breathing.

*This deformed catfish was found in a Georgia stream. All the evidence points to acid rain as the culprit.*

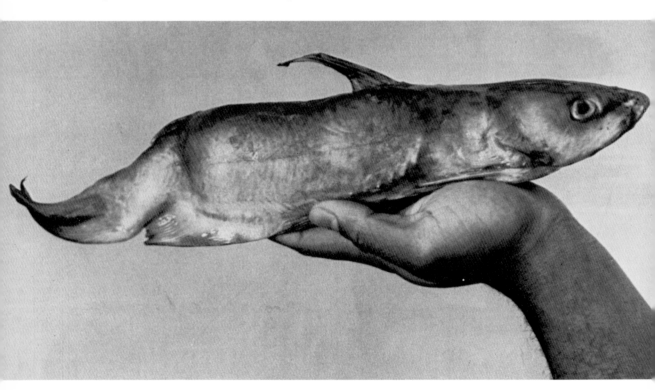

Eventually, as acid levels rise, most forms of life disappear from the lake. The lake becomes beautifully crystal clear. This is because most of the plant life has been destroyed. Often the only life left in an acidified lake is a carpet of algae on the bottom that is resistant to acid.

As to the impact of acid rain on forests and croplands, no one is sure. In some areas, such as forests enshrouded in fog at high altitudes, the damage has been devastating. However, at lower elevations, there has been little, or no, obvious damage. It seems that even acids contain nutrients that the plants can use. Since these acids are absorbed indirectly through the soil and not directly, as with aquatic plants, their toxic effects are lessened. There is some evidence that acid rain is destroying the smaller feeder roots of trees. It will take years, though, to measure the effects of this destruction.

One study by the U.S.-Canadian research group reported that the rate of forest growth is declining in Scandinavia and in the northeastern United States. The results of this decline over the years could prove disastrous to wildlife populations that live in these forests.

In metropolitan areas worldwide, some buildings and monuments are suffering severe damage from acid rain. The Statue of Liberty, in New York City, had to be totally renovated due to acid damage. Cleopatra's Needle, an Egyptian obelisk (pointed pillar) that is approximately 3,500 years old, suffered serious surface damage after being exposed to New York City's rainfall and air pollution while on display there in the 1860s.

Acid rain has affected more than 7,000 lakes in Canada's Ontario province alone. Scientific studies show that this acidic rainfall is shrinking the eastern Canadian duck population, weakening the maple trees, and eating away at marble structures.

Further research has shown that acid rain is also affecting the human population. Studies have demonstrated that commercial fish (fish eaten by humans) from acidified lakes contain high levels of mercury. Tests show that mercury, an element found in nature, reacts with acid rain, changing it to methyl mercury. This form of mercury is especially poisonous to humans.

The face on the Statue of Liberty, even after
renovation, is permanently scarred due to
acid rain and other forms of air pollution.

# THE HYDROLOGIC CYCLE

The *hydrologic cycle* is one of the natural cycles that moves water around the Earth. It works in the following way: The Sun evaporates surface water (water visible on the surface of the Earth) and causes plants to transpire (lose water through openings on the undersides of leaves). This water rises into the atmosphere. As it rises higher, it cools and *condenses* (forms into droplets). These water droplets form into clouds, and the clouds are carried by the wind around the Earth. As the clouds become heavy with condensation, they release their contents as rain, snow, sleet, fog, or hail—all forms of *precipitation*.

## Science Project #9—
## Building an Environment
## for Acid Rain Experiments

### *Materials Needed*

fish tank, 20-gallon capacity or larger
sponge
abrasive cloth
vacuum cleaner
glass piece equal in size to width of tank and one half the tank's height
caulking gun
silicone sealant
gravel
rocks
soil
plants for pond and marsh (elodea, pondweed, cattails, marsh marigolds, arrowheads, or marsh grasses; many of these plants may be obtained from local aquarium stores and garden centers)
water
watering can
glass cover to fit over fish tank
light with 100-watt bulb to go over fish tank
timer

***Observations and Classifications.*** Many of the lakes in the northeastern United States and southeastern Canada have marshes or swamps surrounding them. These lakes and marshes are home to many forms of wildlife. Acid rain now threatens areas such as these.

*Inference.*   Natural cycles can be duplicated in a home or classroom environment.

*Hypothesis.*   If a fish tank is set up like a pond and marsh, then it will simulate many of the cycles found in nature.

*Procedure.*   Clean the fish tank thoroughly, using a sponge and an abrasive cloth. DO NOT USE SOAP. Traces of soap will remain in the tank and alter your natural cycles. Remove all dust and other particles from the tank by vacuuming its bottom and corners.

With the tank clean, you are ready to construct the pond and marsh. In order to separate the pond from the marsh, a glass piece should be placed in the middle of the tank, dividing the tank in half. Using the caulking gun, seal this glass piece in place by running a bead of silicone sealant along the bottom and sides of the center of the tank. Carefully place the glass into the silicone bead and, with your finger, smooth the silicone between the glass piece and the sides of the tank. The silicone, which takes twenty-four hours to cure, will waterproof these sections of the tank and prevent water from seeping through from one section to the other.

After the silicone has cured, cover the bottom areas of both sections with gravel. The gravel should be at least 3 inches thick in the pond portion and 5 inches thick in the marsh section. In the marsh area, the gravel should be sloped from 3 inches deep at the glass divider to 5 inches deep at the back of the tank.

In the marsh area of the tank, put soil and rocks over the gravel. Soil can be obtained from many garden centers. Cover the gravel with soil to 2 inches below the glass divider, in a slight slope, to the rear of the tank. Place rocks at the divider to prevent soil runoff. Rocks may also be placed in other areas of the tank for effect.

Before adding water to the tank, plant your vegetation. The wetland plants, such as the marsh marigolds, marsh grasses, and arrowheads, should be planted in the marsh section. Submerged vegetation, such as elodea and pondweed, should be planted in the pond area.

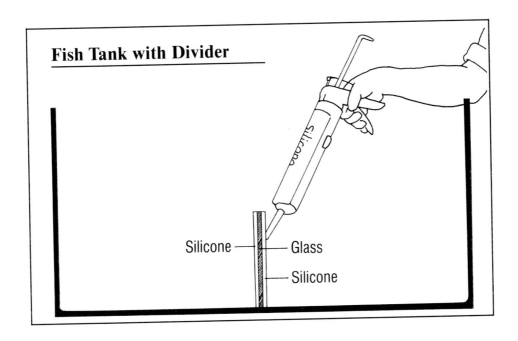

## Fish Tank with Divider

Silicone — Glass

Silicone

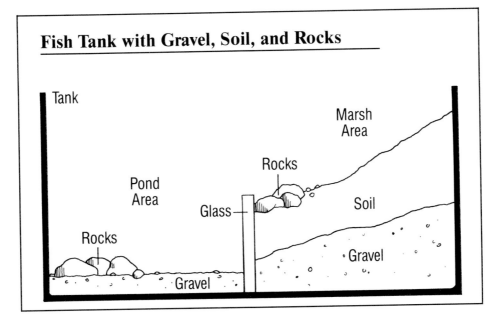

## Fish Tank with Gravel, Soil, and Rocks

Tank

Marsh
Area

Rocks

Pond
Area

Soil

Glass

Rocks

Gravel

Gravel

Fill the pond area with water until there is ½ inch of standing water in the marsh section. This will keep your wetland plants constantly moist.

Lightly water the marsh section of the tank with a watering can. Immediately after watering the marsh, cover the entire tank with a piece of glass sized to fit on top of the tank.

Set up the light over the tank, on a timer set for fifteen hours of light per day. This will simulate June sunlight in the northeastern United States and southeastern Canada.

Use the pond and marsh you set up to study the hydrologic cycle. Observe the tank every day for approximately two weeks. In your results, log evaporation and transpiration (water droplets on leaves). Note the condensation on the glass above. The precipitation will come from these water droplets (which simulate clouds) as they become heavy and fall.

**Results.** 1. It precipitated. 2. There is runoff.

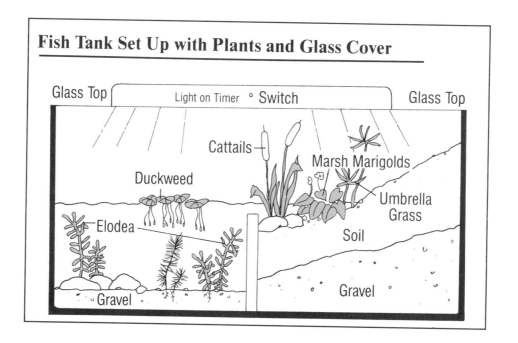

**Fish Tank Set Up with Plants and Glass Cover**

# Sample Log of Hydrologic Cycle

| Day | 1 | 2 | 3 | 4 | 5 | 6 | 7 | 8 | 9 | 10 | 11 | 12 | 13 | 14 |
|---|---|---|---|---|---|---|---|---|---|---|---|---|---|---|
| Evaporation | water vapor rose from the pond 1/6 of an inch | water vapor continues to rise from pond | | | | | | | | | | | | |
| Transpiration | water vapor seemed to escape from plants | water vapor continues to rise from plants | | | | | | | | | | | | |
| Condensation | droplets of water begin to form on glass | droplets of water enlarge, some are heavy | | | | | | | | | | | | |
| Precipitation | | heavy droplets release water, which falls to soil | | | | | | | | | | | | |
| Runoff | | | | | | | | | | | | | | |

**(MAKE YOUR OWN CHART OR PHOTOCOPY THIS ONE.)**

## Science Project #10—
## The Effects of Acid Rain on
## the pH of Water and Soil

### Materials Needed

water pH test kit
pond and marsh environment set
up in Science Project #9
soil pH test kit
vinegar (to simulate sulfuric and
nitric acids)

atomizer bottle with bulb squeeze
pump or handle pump (An
old, cleaned Windex bottle
will do. Be sure to wash the
bottle thoroughly.)

*Observations and Classifications.* Acid rain is caused by nitrogen and sulfur dioxide gases combining with other elements in the atmosphere to create nitric acid and sulfuric acid. These two acids are the main components of acid rain. Information on the effects of these acids in the environment can be obtained by reading earlier sections of this book.

*Prediction.* Acid rain will change the pH of water and soil.

*Hypothesis.* If acid rain falls on a pond or marsh, then it will change the pH of that pond or marsh.

*Procedure.* The first step in this project is to test the water in the pond and marsh for pH. Use your water pH test kit to do this, and record the results. Then test your soil for pH by using the soil test kit. Follow the directions in the kit. Record your results. Test the water and soil every day for one month. This will allow time for normal pH levels to form.

Fill the atomizer with the vinegar (acetic acid). Lift the glass cover on the tank and mist the pond and marsh areas with the vinegar. Also mist the underside of the glass cover. Set the glass cover back on top of the tank.

Repeat this part of the experiment every day for three weeks. During this time, record the pH of the water and the soil every other day.

# Chart of Results

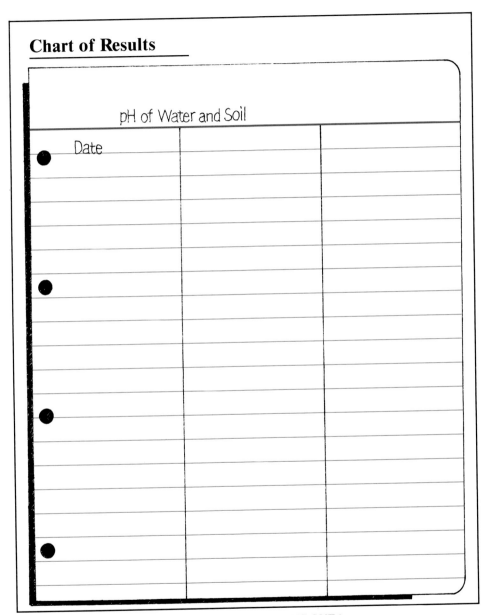

pH of Water and Soil

| Date | | |
|------|---|---|
| | | |
| | | |
| | | |
| | | |
| | | |
| | | |
| | | |
| | | |
| | | |
| | | |
| | | |
| | | |
| | | |
| | | |
| | | |
| | | |
| | | |
| | | |

**(MAKE YOUR OWN CHART OR PHOTOCOPY THIS ONE.)**

## Science Project #11—
## The Effects of Acid Rain
## on Aquatic and Land Vegetation

### Materials Needed

pond and marsh environment set
up in Science Project #9
water pH test kit
soil pH test kit
compound microscope
cover slips
glass slides

atomizer bottle with bulb squeeze
pump or handle pump (An
old, cleaned Windex bottle
will do. Be sure to wash the
bottle thoroughly.)
vinegar (to simulate sulfuric and
nitric acid)

(NOTE: This project should be done simultaneously with Science Project
#10 for best results.)

**Observations and Classifications.**   Observations and classifications for
this project have been obtained by reading the earlier sections in this
chapter.

**Prediction.**   Acid rain will damage aquatic and land vegetation.

**Hypothesis.**   If vegetation is exposed to acid rain, then it will be dam-
aged or destroyed.

**Procedure.**   Take a leaf from an elodea plant (or from another submerged pond plant) and place it on a glass slide. Cover the leaf gently
with a cover slip. DO NOT PRESS DOWN. Place the slide on the stage
of a compound microscope, focus, and examine the leaf.

(NOTE: If you are not familiar with the operation of a compound microscope, ask your teacher or the school's science teacher to help you with
this part of the project.)

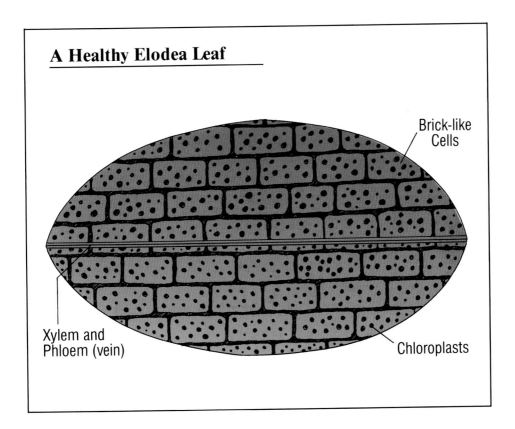

**A Healthy Elodea Leaf**

Brick-like Cells

Xylem and Phloem (vein)

Chloroplasts

The leaf should be filled with bricklike cells, and each cell will be filled with *chloroplasts* (tiny disks that contain a green substance called *chlorophyll*). Chlorophyll is the only substance on Earth that can take light energy and transform it into chemical energy, which the plant then uses to make food. If the plant did not contain chlorophyll, it would not be able to make food. Diagram the leaf as under the microscope and label its parts.

In your results, record the state of health of the pond and marsh vegetation. Write down whether the plants are turgid (firm) and green (filled with chlorophyll).

Spray acetic acid on the aquatic environment as was directed in Science Project #10. Do this every other day for three weeks. Each day record the results. At the end of three weeks, remove another elodea leaf and examine it under the microscope. Diagram the leaf and answer the following questions: How does this leaf compare in turgidity and in the shape of its cells to the same leaf as it was three weeks ago? Is the amount of chlorophyll in each cell the same?

Continue the experiment and diagram the leaf again in three weeks.

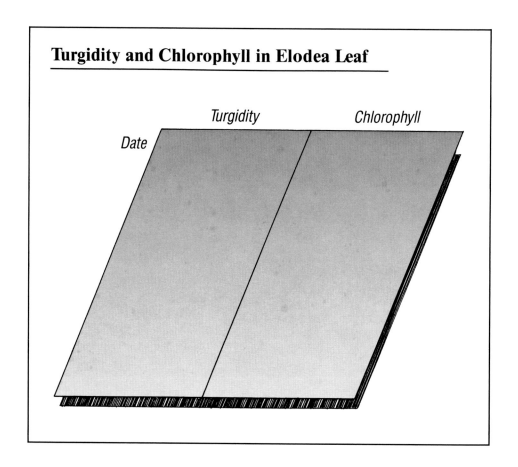

**Turgidity and Chlorophyll in Elodea Leaf**

Date    Turgidity    Chlorophyll

# 6

## *What Can Be Done About Acid Rain?*

The acid rain problem is growing. Right now, the hardest hit areas of the world are parts of Scandinavia, the United States, and Canada. The pollution, however, is spreading. Very soon, additional parts of these countries and currently unaffected countries will begin to experience the same devastation, because we have not acted to reduce the emissions of sulfur dioxide and nitrogen oxides into the atmosphere.

Stopping acid rain will require international cooperation. All countries, industries, and people must work together to achieve the goal of clean air and water. Reducing our dependence on fossil fuels (coal, oil, and natural gas) is the best, and probably the only reasonable, way to halt the spread of acid rain.

Industries must become more fuel efficient and must produce cleaner and fewer emissions. Transportation systems must be redesigned to use smaller amounts of cleaner burning fuels. Laws must be passed that will require industries to use cleaner fuels and to produce fewer emissions.

Recently, the U.S. government passed a new Clean Air Act, which is expected to help with the problem of acid rain. Because of this act, emissions should drop by half by the year 2000. The effects should be felt in Canada within ten to fifteen years. Some researchers believe that the lakes will go back to their natural, healthy state. This remains to be seen.

Of course, changes are costly. Many say that it will cost too much to develop pollution-free technologies. The cost, however, of not doing anything will far surpass the costs of solving the problem. The cost of air and water pollution to industries such as commercial fishing, forestry, and tourism will be huge. The loss of natural resources will eventually put existing industries out of business. Finally, energy depletion will threaten many industries and communities.

## WHAT CAN YOU DO?

We must all try to protect the natural resources of this planet. You can do your part by taking an active role in seeing that changes are made. Write letters to your local and state representatives and to the federal government. Ask that stricter legislation on acid rain be passed. Write letters to newspapers and industry leaders. Organize groups to study the problem, and investigate ways to deal with it. You can also do your part to preserve our natural resources by conserving energy and recycling materials.

Your scientific investigation of acid rain need not stop here. What we have done in this book is only a beginning. Read more about the problem and about the science related to it. Make up your own experiments. Enter science fairs with projects on acid rain. See what new solutions you can devise. The future is up to you. Take the initiative to get things started. Even a small step forward is a step in the right direction.

*We must try to protect all the resources on our planet, including the wildlife.*

## Conclusions
## to
## Projects

2. My hypothesis was correct because all ecosystems have food webs for transferring energy.
3. My hypothesis was correct because acids do turn blue litmus paper red, bases do turn red litmus paper blue, and neutral substances do not change either litmus paper at all.
4. My hypothesis was correct because acetic acid combined with sodium hydroxide did neutralize each other and form salt plus water.
5. My hypothesis was correct because acid did corrode the tile and some, though not all, of the other substances.
6. My hypothesis was correct because, when the sulfur was burned, the paper changed from white to gray, indicating that the sulfur combined with oxygen in the air to form sulfur dioxide gas.
7. My hypothesis was correct because the litmus paper changed color, indicating that the vapor was acidic. Therefore, when sulfur dioxide gas combined with water vapor, it formed sulfuric acid.
8. My hypothesis was correct because the rainfall did measure 3.5 to 5.5 on the pH scale.
9. My hypothesis was correct because the hydrologic cycle could be artificially created in a fish tank.
10. My hypothesis was correct because the acid rain did change the pH of the marsh.
11. My hypothesis was correct because the acid rain did damage the vegetation.

# *For*
# *Further*
# *Information*

## Government Agencies

Environmental Protection Agency (EPA)
Public Information Center
401 M Street SW
Washington, DC 20460
202-475-7751

National Environmental Satellite Data
  and Information Service
1825 Connecticut Avenue
Washington, DC 20235
202-673-5594

## Consumer Groups

Environmental Action Foundation
724 Dupont Circle Building NW
Washington, DC 20036
202-745-4871

Environmental Defense Fund
1525 18th Street NW
Washington, DC 20036
202-387-3500

Worldwatch Institute
1776 Massachusetts Avenue
Washington, DC 20046
202-452-1999

## Books

*Acid Rain Reader.* Raleigh, NC: Acid Rain Foundation, 1987.

Asimov, Isaac. *How Did We Find Out About the Atmosphere?* New York: Walker & Co. 1985.

Corson, Walter H. *The Global Ecology Handbook.* New York: Global Tomorrow Coalition, 1990.

Earth Works Group. *50 Simple Things Kids Can Do To Save the Earth.* Kansas City, MO: Earthworks Press, 1990.

Gutnik, Martin J. *The Challenge of Clean Air.* Hillside, NJ: Enslow Publishers, Inc., 1990.

Neiburger, Melvin. *Understanding Our Atmosphere's Environment.* New York: W. H. Freeman, 1982.

# *Glossary*

**Acid.** Any substance that has a sour taste, turns blue litmus paper red, contains hydrogen, and is corrosive. Acids usually measure below 7.0 on the pH scale.

**Acid Rain.** Rainwater containing acids that have formed from the combination of sulfur dioxide, nitric oxide, or nitrogen dioxide with water vapor.

**Alkaline.** Describes any substance having a pH greater than 7.0, such as a base.

**Ammonium Hydroxide ($NH_4OH$).** A colorless, basic solution of ammonia ($NH_3$) in water.

**Base.** Any substance that has a bitter taste, is slippery to the touch, contains a hydroxyl (OH), and turns red litmus paper blue. Bases usually measure above 7.0 on the pH scale.

**Biological.** Refers to any currently living, once living, or future living thing.

**Biosphere.** The portion of the Earth and its atmosphere that is capable of supporting life.

**Calcium Hydroxide ($Ca(OH)_2$).** A soft white powder used in making mortar and cement; also called "slaked lime" or limewater when in solution (water). Used in scientific experiments as a carbon dioxide indicator.

**Carbon Dioxide ($CO_2$).** A colorless, odorless, tasteless gas found naturally in small amounts in the air.

**Carnivore.** Any animal that eats only meat.

**Cell.** The smallest unit of living matter.

**Chlorophyll.** A green substance found in plants; it is the only substance known that can convert light energy into chemical energy, or food.

**Chloroplasts.** Tiny, disk-shaped objects found in the cells of plants; chloroplasts contain the substance chlorophyll.

**Classification.** The grouping of objects according to their properties.

**Conclusion.** The gathering and interpreting of data in a scientific experiment, to find out if your hypothesis was correct or incorrect.

**Condensation.** The changing of water vapor (a gas) into droplets of liquid water.

**Controlled Experiment.** An experiment in which variables are manipulated to bring about measurable results.

**Corrosive.** Describes any substance capable of dissolving or wearing away other substances, especially metals.

**Deposition.** Refers to the falling of acid rain and dry particles from polluting emissions.

**Detritus Food Web.** Food relationships among the consumers of decaying or waste material; the process by which nutrients from dead and waste material are returned to the environment.

**Ecology.** The study of how all living things interrelate with each other and with their nonliving environment.

**Ecosystem.** A specialized community, including all of its various organisms, that functions as an interacting system; one example is a bog.

**Emission.** The release of waste products during the combustion of fossil fuels.

**Evaporation.** The process of water rising into the air as a gas, water vapor.

**Food Web.** See **Detritus Food Web** and **Grazing Food Web.**

**Fossil Fuel.** Any fuel formed from the fossil remains of plants or animals, for example, coal, oil, and natural gas.

**Glucose.** A simple sugar made by plants during the process of photosynthesis.

**Grazing Food Web.** Also called the *food chain;* a way of transferring and transforming solar energy for use by a variety of organisms within a community.

**Herbivore.** Any animal that eats only vegetation.

**Hydrogen Sulfide ($H_2S$).** A noxious, foul-smelling gas that naturally rises over swamps and marshes as the result of decomposing organic matter. It is also produced by some industrial processes.

**Hydrologic Cycle.** The regular movement of water from the atmosphere, by precipitation, to the Earth's surface and its return to the atmosphere, by evaporation and transpiration.

**Hydroxyl (OH).** A combination of an oxygen (O) atom and a hydrogen (H) atom chemically bound together.

**Hypothesis.** An educated guess formed from the observations and classifications concerning a scientific experiment or problem; an inference or a prediction that can be tested.

**Inference.** An educated guess based on what has been observed about an event.

**Leaching.** Refers to nutrients and metals being washed from the Earth; acid rain leaches nutrients from the soil.

**Limewater.** See **Calcium Hydroxide.**

**Mercury (Hg).** A silvery white, poisonous, metallic element that is liquid at room temperature.

**Natural Pollution.** Refers to pollution by nature through its natural cycles.

**Neutralization.** Refers to when an acid and a base react together to form a salt plus water.

**Nitrogen (N).** A gas that makes up 78 percent of our air.

**Nitrogen Oxides.** Mainly nitric oxide (NO) and nitrogen dioxide ($NO_2$), which are ingredients of acid rain.

**Observation.** A method, using the five senses, of studying scientific or natural phenomena.

**Omnivore.** Any animal that eats both plants and meat.

**Oxygen (O).** A gas that makes up about 21 percent of our air.

**pH.** Refers to how acidic or alkaline a substance is, measured on a scale ranging from 0 to 14.

**Photosynthesis.** The process by which green plants make food.

**Precipitation.** Water falling to Earth as rain, snow, sleet, hail, or fog.

**Prediction.** An educated guess, based on observation, about something that is going to happen.

**Property.** Something that belongs to an object that helps us to identify that object; objects have physical and chemical properties.

**Results.** The record of what happened during a scientific investigation or experiment.

**Sulfur (S).** A pale yellow, nonmetallic element found widely in nature.

**Sulfur Dioxide ($SO_2$).** A compound formed both naturally and by the combustion of coal or oil, both of which contain sulfur; when combined with water vapor, sulfur dioxide forms sulfuric acid, an ingredient of acid rain.

**Sulfuric Acid ($H_2SO_4$).** An acid formed when sulfur dioxide gas combines with water vapor; it is the main ingredient in acid rain.

**Toxic.** Poisonous.

**Transpiration.** Loss of water from plants; plants transpire water into the air through openings on the undersides of their leaves.

**Variables.** Differing conditions (such as temperature, time of day, and amount of sunlight) that might affect the outcome of a scientific investigation or experiment.

**Water Vapor.** Water in the form of a gas; water in the air.

**Wet Deposition.** Refers to acid precipitation (such as rain, snow, sleet, hail, or fog).

# *Index*

## *About the Author*

Martin J. Gutnik received his bachelor of science and master of science degrees from the University of Wisconsin. He is currently a sixth-grade teacher and an elementary school science specialist in Wisconsin. He was the Elementary Science Program coordinator for Shorewood Public Schools from 1970 to 1986, and since 1973 he has also been the Shorewood Public Schools Environmental System director.

Mr. Gutnik has been a prolific author of science books for children throughout his career. He has published many titles for Franklin Watts, Children's Press, and Enslow Publications. He has written articles for the *World Book* encyclopedia and *The New Book of Knowledge* and has authored teachers' manuals and student workbooks for the State of Wisconsin Department of Public Instruction's *Process-Oriented Science* series for first through third grades.

Mr. Gutnik is married and has four children.